# Contents

MICHELLE SMITH

*dear Hermes...*

The University of Alberta Press

Published by
The University of Alberta Press
Ring House 2
Edmonton, Alberta, Canada  T6G 2E1
www.uap.ualberta.ca

LIBRARY AND ARCHIVES CANADA CATALOGUING IN PUBLICATION

Smith, Michelle, 1974–
    Dear Hermes— / Michelle Smith.

(Robert Kroetsch series of Canadian creative works)
Poems.
ISBN 978-0-88864-597-5

    I. Title  II. Series: Robert Kroetsch series of Canadian creative works.

PS8637.M56525D43 2012    C811'.6    C2012-900190-2

First edition, first printing, 2012.
Printed and bound in Canada by Houghton Boston Printers, Saskatoon, Saskatchewan.
Copyediting and proofreading by Alice Major.

A volume in the Robert Kroetsch series.

The University of Alberta Press gratefully acknowledges the support received for its publishing program from The Canada Council for the Arts. The University of Alberta Press also gratefully acknowledges the financial support of the Government of Canada through the Canada Book Fund (CBF) and the Government of Alberta through the Alberta Multimedia Development Fund (AMDF) for its publishing activities.

 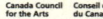

*For Matt and Dashiell*

*dear Hermes...*

dear Hermes—

no stars danced at my birth.

hospital fluorescent chilled
my blood-slicked skin, and what child
wouldn't howl and beat her fists
against that false light?

not like you, born in a mist, born laughing
at the joke you never told to anyone, not even me,
your mercurial daughter with eyes as bright
as an equinox eclipse, as mutable as
the poison liquid beads I dreamt

a multitude of ravens gathered together
        and let spill as silver beads
                across the night skies.

when they laughed, those stars flickered
and you
vanished into ink-cloud and constellation.

a responsible father, you left me your tortoiseshell lyre,
gold coins stolen from silk merchants, and the legacy
of your god's sunlit skin, yet—

it is the pen I pilfered from the Muses
that makes me laugh

and if I'm caught siphoning the songs of Helicon,
then you'll have some explaining to do
because I'm as good as you
at vanishing acts, and though my sleight-of-hand life
is as unsteady as a drunken butcher's dance.

I stole, too, your love of words
as smooth and sleek as raven's wings,
as indigo and flame.

dear Dionysus—

if you gave me half a chance, I would weep merlot
and love for you; I would cherish nakedness and frenzy.

I declare myself double-bound by birth and tragedy,
and if you're out there and you're listening, Dionysus,
you ought to seek me out here, at the edge of disbelief,
this place where no one believes in maenads or myths.

I'll be the girl writing postcards backwards with a mirror
because it's as good a way to kill time before dying as any.

I'll be the girl imagining a future so far in the past
we ought to hold a funeral for its departure.

3

dear Chronos—

how do you tell time here?

by the sound of waves,
of water slipping up and washing away,
eternal return?

or by the sand slipping endlessly out from under your feet?

or by the gap in blues: sky-cloud-sea; sea-cloud-sky?

or do you tell it by the undertow?


I imagine you'd reply enigmatically,
like an oracle suffering from sleep deprivation,
or a muse with a sore throat.

you leave me with nothing but poetry:
the art of crafting galleries from words and memory,
an architecture of elegant symbols made
from blue liquid stroked across white paper,
and beloved lists of all the things I love and fear to forget.

you leave me with nothing but 12.12.12:
midnight on the twelfth of December.

The words for star, love, hunger.
All sunk deep in the Atlantic.

Their friends, their village, their farm.

All as good as drowned.

The story of my great-great-grandparents
is hidden in the domain of Hades and Persephone,
whose realm must resemble a great library
of lost tales that is more vast than even the prairies
and their wild leaping from one horizon to the next.

Disguised by the flat fields are the depths
that lurk beneath, the dark depths
that conceal the bones of my ancestors
in their unmarked settlers' graves.

My family has searched for these graves,
searched for words to describe such loss,
but I suspect it's better this way, the past
untouchable, incorporeal.

What name, after all,
could have been chiselled
into stone for us to trace
with our fingertips?

Upon their arrival,
they were stripped
as bare as corpses,
all the thunder and ferocity
of their Nordic name, *Thorbjornsen*
muted and tamed.
Anglicized:
*Thompson*, a name
full of spectres
and doubt.

is the heady inhalation of creosote,
deep into the lungs. The taste of it
rolling over the tongue. The way it turns
distances into a limpid summer haze.

6

It's the way the three of us loved to tempt Fate,
running down the middle of the tracks
as a black engine gunned and smoked
behind us, its whistle shrieking
like a banshee. And it's the stories
we were told of bays and blacks
and appaloosas who roamed
the farmland before it was farmland,
and it's the memory
of interminable drives to visit relatives
in one-horse-towns-that-the-horse-had-left,
the three of us sticking to the cheap vinyl
of station wagon's back seat.

It's the memory of killing time,
because there was time,
and there was time,
so much time.

Lying heavy
like great swaths
of severed wheat
in our small hands.

Especially at night.

Listening to the rattling of our bedroom windows,
imagining the trains departing
in clouds of throat-thickening dust,
leaving us behind, leaving us
sweating in the heat, leaving us feeling
the rustling ache and sway of fields
under the harvest moon.

Some nights, fear closed in,
gripping us with that ache.

Fear of the ache of old age, creeping
into our knees and hobbling us, tilting
our backs forward to see our own shuffling feet,
only our own shuffling feet.

The surest escape
was waking early
and walking to the tracks,
following them
as far was we dared
and looking off
into the crisp cool distances of dawn,
then listing out loud
the names of our favourite foreign destinations:
Paris—Athens—Cairo—Istanbul—Oslo—Rome.

Looking east, we forgot
the vanished horses
the bent backs
the haze and the ache
and the way these things
were always threatening
to grind themselves
down into our very bones,
into the twist and jackknife
of our every breath.

8

My grandmother comes back to me
in scattered images
that resemble the dappled sunlight
passing through the cherry blossoms
outside her living room window,
patterning my hands as I curled
on her sofa one summer, writing endless stories
about horses named Moonshine and Aurora
or drawing pictures of the stray cats
she let me feed in the alley behind her garden.

*This one's gifted, she is.*
*Look at this drawing, just read this story!*
Her gnarled voice leaps across a dozen years
with the sight of her freckled, bony hands
holding up my fragile creations to her friends.
And there I stand, in memory too,
suntanned and dusty, looking down
at my bare feet, the right sole
covering the top of the left,
my hands clasped behind my back.

By her kitchen window, eating egg on toast,
I would kick the legs of my chair, absently,
or watch the robins make nests in the trees,
writing horse stories in my mind
while she told me about her parent's emigration
from Norway and described the antics
of Clarence, her orange tabby cat
who had to be put to sleep
because he just got too old and incontinent,
kept peeing in the flower bed
*I couldn't figure out why my lilies kept dying*
she chuckled, then sighed.
*Sometimes I forget he's gone and put milk out for him.*

The next summer brought the obliterating glare
of the hospital, sirens wailing in my ears
along with the adult warning that my grandmother
might no longer recognize me. As I stood by her bed,
she took my hand, winked and murmured
*why don't you write me a story or two*
*about a cat named Clarence.*

9

*Spent the thirties riding the rails. Wound up at a lumber camp. Took my place along*
*the log chute after lunch that first day. There was blood everywhere. I said: Hey, why*
*is there blood everywhere? Guy further up the line, real joker, says: That's what's left*
*of the guy who had your job this morning.*

A raw badlands day in late September, my young skin
feeling stretched and scratched by the wind
as I stand with his battered old notebook
concealed in the pocket of my coat.

Brother, father, grandfather.
The titles spiral out
from the funeral wreath
on maroon ribbons.

No heart attack, whatever my parents claimed.

His veins were so full of alcohol
that on his death-day he lit a match
to light a cigarette, and ignited instead
his heart.

*They made me a medic in '42. The headlines called it The Road to Rome!*
*Like it was a fairy tale, all Judy Garland and red ruby shoes.*
*I have nothing to say about that war. Nothing.*

Pinpricks of snow flick at my face,
the minister's voice a distant lull,
—*ashes to ashes, dust to dust*—
and I am thinking of the sparks
I am sure are still in his blood,
glowing bright and exclamatory.

*Ran the coal mine after I got back.*
*Lost my hearing blasting through rock.*

And I want so badly to see
smoke creeping out,
all of the adults growing
dazed and confused and
—WHOOMP—
the man the town called
the dynamite man
suddenly sets himself ablaze,
to billow up
like a Roman emperor,
transformed by inferno,
made royal and ascendant.

i.

For twenty years
he has arrived home every day
at five-thirty, has crowded his truck
into the two-car garage
beside his wife's VW.
Twenty years. Every day.

Today he steps over the pool of slick-sticky oil
that has taken the place of his wife's car.
Pausing, he listens for the sound
of his daughter at the piano.
*A sadist!* he always yells upon entering the house,
deflecting her efforts to make
Beethoven and Bartok smash open his skull.
He tries to make it funny, to ignore his sense
of the hairs on the back of her neck standing on end
when he enters, his sense of her obliterating
his absent-minded cruelties
with her *fortissimo, sforzando.*

At five-thirty-two today, he stands on the threshold,
calls out *hallo,* and then, again
*Hallo?*
*Is anybody there?*

He slips off his shoes, paces through hallway, den, kitchen,
searching for a note. She is always leaving notes. His wife.
Drives him crazy. Requests and reminders
scratched on scrap paper, scattered all over the house,
the air devoid of her cracked voice, her silences
leaching at them both. Now there is not even a note.
Only the clean, dark plane of the mahogany dining table.
He sits down in his usual place at the head of the table.

He waits,
and the house waits with him.

He watches ·
the day drain itself into twilight, then night.
Time to call the police yet?
Panic, yet?
He remembers that his wife has a cousin in the RCMP.
He remembers the hollowed-out spaces
beneath his wife's cheekbones, the darkness underneath her eyes.

He waits,
while across the city,
his daughter is sitting on a bed in a cheap motel
glaring with intensity at the movie *Amadeus*.

Her fingers intertwine,
a white knot of bones straining against skin
while her mother's voice rattles on
and rattles off against her skull
and a red neon sign flashes *vacancy*
across her white-as-a-sheet cheek.

switzer, yes switzer is the name i'll use
he'll never think of it
my great-grandmother's name
do you like it
sitting there silent and sullen
as always you are
an ungrateful bitch
all of this i'm doing for you
leaving like this it's a terrible risk
and what do I get for it you wretch

oh my beautiful daughter
the smart one you always were
you could talk at six months
read at two and a half and
it was miraculous  you were my miracle
you rotten snotty little

my god i can't tell if i said that out loud
can you hear me i can't tell
are you listening oh my beautiful smart baby
who stole all the words always talking
always fighting
*why don't you just get a divorce*
you asked *mommy please can we go?*
you were only three goddammit
how did you learn the word divorce by three?

but now which words are inside my head
which ones am i saying out loud i used
to keep them so straight, so separate

there's no air in here
i'll open a window    there    that's better
         please listen to me
         damn you  i gave you life
listen to me  maybe we could go to Victoria
      i've always loved Victoria
                  i haven't been there since before i got married
         look at me not that damned tv  damn your eyes.
they are his


      they are his
            always watching without looking like you're looking
it's not your fault
            that you have the eyes of the devil
                  so I will protect you
         oh, a mother's love
      you wouldn't believe its power    i will protect you
like a bear I am a bear dear i am a bear

iii.

and what could I do, coming home
from school on a Wednesday afternoon
and finding the car crammed with suitcases—

> *we're leaving your father*, she says
> *you have fifteen minutes to pack*
> *whatever you think you want to keep*

and all I can think of is the piano.
at least, the music books? *no, there isn't room.*
*be practical.* I grab some clothes, babysitting money
and sneak in Sonata no. 14, *Quasi Una Fantasia.*

she speeds through school zones, runs red lights,
the car jerking wildly when she changes gears.
I grip the door handle until my hand cramps.
I listen to symphonies inside my head to block her voice,
to balance the sickening arrhythmia of the car—

*i wouldn't be surprised* she says *if your father smashed*
*that piano in a rage when he finds us gone.*
*but i'll protect you like a mother bear*, she says.

she says a lot of things.

I am saved from hearing them by Bartok's *Bear's Dance*
beating out a rhythm between my temples
as we gain momentum, as she hurls us
headlong into a sunset that lights the city on fire.
then, our speed evens out.
we are on a highway of bloodied carcasses,
of smashed muskrats and magpies.

then there is a train of motels. a coil of false names.
cash. everything is paid for in cash,
and we always check out before breakfast,
always hungry, and after three weeks
I start to laugh at things not funny,
like gophers with flies where their eyes should be
and the sign on one bed: *Magic Fingers, 5 Cents.*

and after six weeks,
she takes me
home
again.

dear Hera—

where were you, o goddess of hearth and home?

I'll tell you where you were: always away, chasing after Zeus,
cursing white cows and setting snakes on newborn boys.
O! how you suffered. yes, you: a goddess.

while here we were, that whole time. my two sisters, my mother,
and I. And the series of men who, liking the eyes of my mother,
lied and said they'd shelter us from the wind whipping up the fields,
from the stinging dead-earth dance of windstorms and dust.

but you couldn't be bothered with this place, could you?
and who could blame you. So far, so very far from your home,
and so cold, too. no wine, no olives; no sea and certainly no temples.
no gods, evidently.

all that is left of that time is the frame of our old farmhouse, collapsing.
when the roof finally gives, all that will remain
is a dead hearth of stone, cold as the heart of my abandoned mother.

O! you'd say (if I bothered to ask) how your heart bled
time and again, sides splitting from chasing Zeus.

but I won't ask, for I've long known that you never, ever
spared a thought for all of those women who were chased,
who found themselves cornered on the far side of a dining table,
or who ran panicking into the fields, or sometimes into rivers.

curse you, you and your resplendent peacock.

all of those glorious eyes, not one of them able to see.

Ugly hands. Peasant hands,
immigrant hands: stubby fingers
and broken nails. Blue veins,
but no bloodlines.

Palm pressed to palm,                                                    19
the resemblance
was so clear
it was as if a sculptor
had made us both from marble.

Whatever grace our hands shared took shape
in waves of ink over the blank page,
in the elegance of the slanted script I learned
in imitation of her, my lone imagination soaring
in letters keen as the cries of seabirds
in the blue and white of ocean crashing on rock.

Her hands preferred knitting,
crossword puzzles, the dignity of nail files.
Words were monsters best kept hidden under the bed,
and the miracle of her fingerprints matching
the imprint of mine was nothing
but a trick of evolution,
and cruel.

## Obscurity

(*Portrait of the Artist's Mother.* 1629, Jan Lievens)

I doubt she was ever obscure to herself,
this woman Jan Lievens painted
as a figure sunk on all sides
into encroaching shadows,
making me feel he was folding up
his own fear of her death
into the folds of her black cloak.

He painted her reading all alone,
which of course makes such a thing impossible.
For his painting is an invitation
to others to stand in his place
and let their presence become
nothing more, or less,
than the continuation of hers.

Another of his painter's tricks—
he made light appear to leap
from the pages of the book
that his mother holds so close to her face,
illuminating the lovely translucence of her skin
as the edges of the parchment curve up, so gently,
to touch, nearly but not quite,
the face he made immortal.

The story changes with each telling,
gathering force over time the way a flood swells
until it is capable of sweeping away the foundations of bridges.

In the wake of this particular flood,
a flotsam of altarpieces, a jetsam of triptychs
have been rescued, as if they are children adrift, crying out.

Try to grasp them, and they just might pull you under.
Me, I'm nothing but an empty lifeboat, floating,
along with the waves of tourists, to see Mary.

She has stood still for six centuries,
folds of gold draped all around her,
though darkness remains:
the thundercloud beneath
Gabriel's feet, the blue
of the dove at her ear.

She stands, reaching with one hand as if
to hold her place in her book. She raises
her other hand as if she could silence such a messenger.

The story changes with each telling, for it reverberates
only briefly in each listener's ear, then leaves it empty,
as empty as the hands of a virgin.

21

(1430, Fra Angelico)

I glimpse it first
when I'm three steps up the flight
of stairs that lead to the monks' cells
painted by Fra Angelico.

22    A fresco I fell for years ago.
This is the painting I have dreamed, schemed,
sacrificed, and saved up to see:
the book of hours on Mary's knee,
its pages paler than doves, and the sharp, white dove
suspended in a shaft of light.
The blue ceiling lit by gold pinprick stars.
The spangled garb of an Archangel.

At the top of the stairs, I pause to take it in.
And giggle. I'm unable to stop myself from thinking
*The Devil is in the Details.*

A kind of sacrilege, no doubt, that giggle.
That thought.

Because it's so sad, after all,
whether you believe any
of the story or not,
it's so sad the way it still makes sense,
how all the details still add up six centuries later:
the way young women are hassled
when they'd rather be left alone,
the way angels can never be relied upon
to show up when you want them,
the way the news of a impending child
always leaves its mother-to-be stunned, wondering—
*But How Can This Be?*

dear Arno—

We both know that no one can step in the same river twice
but then my feet have travelled further and further
each time we meet, and each time I believe
that I am coming home to you.                                    23

You remind me of that other river,
the deepest of them all, the one freighted
with all of the warnings of my childhood:
the Current Swift, the Water Deep: to Sip is Lethal.

Yet I adored the way she always laughed at my little jokes,
how her smile was the patter of rain on new leaves,
her rollicking roar a thunder crash called Avalanche.
Would she remember how I,
a little glittering girl, half-starlight and half-song,
chatted the ferryman into telling me all his tales
while she buoyed the dead, all those dead, clutching
coins in cold palms, cutting half-moons across their life-lines?

Now, dear Arno, you are whispering to me that the solidity
of a city is an act of darkness and imagination.
I look up to see my star, winking like laughter
among old gods and cold clouds

Tired in the early morning light,
I venture out of doors.

White like paper, my skin,
photosensitive, surrenders to
the sensation of sun, to how it feels
to be leaves and bark and blossoms.

I return home with fragments
of an Okanagan orchard laden
with fruit, fill a white bowl on my desk
as sunlight filters through the branches
outside my window and reflects off the burnished wood
of my desk. I begin the search for words to describe
the colours of these fruit, but the scent of peaches
and the taste of cherries linger on my tongue,
leaving the alchemy of words simmering
quietly in the background
of what, already, is.

24

At awkward-stacked altars of books,
we are always kneeling.

We can't help it, can't help ourselves,
the way we are always seeking, seeking.

25

Desire hanging over us like a thousand parched angels.

For those angels to speak, we are always waiting.

Their throats are as dry as old vellum; our ears
are ringing with the agony of patience.

i.

*∴the angels whisper amongst themselves—*

On the first night, Saint Michael the Archangel—he of the Sword and the Dragon—appeared before Aubert and said: *Fear not, for this is to be a Holy Place, made so by Your Hand, for you will build on this island a fortress that bears My name.* And Aubert, afraid, believed it was a dream, and did not act. On the second night, the Michael appeared and commanded him again. And Aubert, still afraid, turned away and did not answer. On the third night, Michael appeared, reached forth and touched the forehead of Aubert, saying *So You Shall Remember*, and Aubert awoke to find a space—golden, pulsating—seared into his skull. This is faith: an island obscured by the fury of the sea, a fortress edged by quicksand.

*…the archivists annotate among whispering papers—*

Mont-Saint-Michel came to be known as the City of Books during the Middle Ages. Its scriptorium became famous for its manuscripts of magnificent full-page illustrations, complete with illuminated letters. The scriptorium went into decline with the creation of the universities, but the manuscripts were preserved at the Mont until 1939, when they were moved to the mainland for safe-keeping and subsequently burned to ash in a blitzkrieg attack.

*…the authors appeal to the angels, give thanks to the archivists, murmuring—*

The tide is a galloping herd of horses, all foam manes & snorting nostrils & salted hoofs…. The sand sinks for the quick & the damned alike…. The medieval pilgrims told one another that crossing the bay was the soul's journey towards Heaven as the Devil sucked at their heels & once a woman went into labour in the bay as the tide swooped towards her & she prayed & she prayed & she prayed until the angels swept down and parted the waves…. The monks built a great cross, *La Croix des Grèves*, to mark the birthplace of this baby born of salt & water…. Over time, the cross sank down, sank down, sank down, into the treacherous embrace of sand.

26

ii.

*ocean /michel    o, san michel*

Archangel of bloodletting and light

you left a shred of your travelling cloak
and the fragrance of roses on the salt air.

You became a love affair, that twist of blood
against the heart: this pilgrimage,

to this place of stone and saltwater and silence.
I ask: who are you? And because you do not answer

I will tell you: you are the glow of red, and I am

the stained glass shards of saintly cloaks; you are
the gleam of green, and I am the scales of painted dragons;

you are the warmth of feather-white and I am the pale hands
of martyred girls whose golden halos grow thinner each year

as gravity pulls thickness into their glass hems.


*o, san michel     ocean/michel*

I am the starry ache of scribal eyes, the scratch of ink & paper,
the songs of lazuli birds among twisted ink branches. I am

a heart caught in the black ash antlers of etched deer.

pause before brushing
the green insect from the page.
pause to spare a thought
for those small lives,
unfolding,
28      camouflaged,
among the leaves
and bird-chirp and
flit of wing.

             pause for feathers
among sweeping leaves, their swaying
swish the song of summer
in full swing beneath the benign
culmination of cumulus clouds
in full swell.
            *pause.*
               caw of crow,
gunmetal sheen of wing seen in the green,
glimpse of gold-amber glow of eye and beak,
infamous devourer of death, whisperer of wisdom
into the ears of gods whose hearths
were the aurora borealis until engines
and exhaust streaked the sky.

beyond the trees, those engines boom
through the sound barrier, leave a suck-shock
that rattles the drum of the ear.

and beyond the garden gate, down in the valley,
there is the endless click-clock-clacking of the trains.

green and gentle,
infinitely ephemeral,
the insect pauses
on the page.

amid the monotony
of machines,
its wings:
soft as rain.

This rubble of marble is a script,
the walls un-scrolling like a lost mother-tongue
written into the hills of Acrocorinth.

Lost cities and fragments of myths
speak of the true order of the universe—
the arbitrary assignment
of fortunes and fates,
the need for temples, for stone
to be hewn and honed into patterns
then doused in fragrant oils
and filled with supplicants.

This temple, here, was once the realm of Aphrodite,
whose tears, they say, fell from the sky
and became the first pearls,
making it possible to steal love from the sea
and lace it on a loop for the neck, to keep love
from slipping off in the undertow,
keep it steady yet shimmering
in the half-moon hollow
at the base of the throat.

i. Black olives and Beaujolais

I have been taught that the Devil covers his cloven hooves
with black leather boots. That he wobbles when he walks
and can't sit steady because of his barbed tail.

30                                                  I have been taught
to feel his skull for the stumps of hidden horns,
to sniff his breath for sulphur and cheap vodka and stale suffering.

But when the Devil smiles, his lips are a soft curve
the colour of Provençal aperitif. He wears linen shirts
as snowy-white-soft as the wings of his lofty brothers. He leaves
his collar open at the throat and his voice travels in waves
of heat that gather in the ear, thick as sticky hot honey.

                                                  I wait
for his eyes to betray him with memories of delight at Dachau,
or raucous laughter over small children
trapped in burning stairwells.

Yet his irises are as clear as the painfully blue Vaucluse sky,
a tragedy of azure grace.

When he rubs the print of his thumb against my lower lip
there is no taste of soot and tar, only black olives and Beaujolais
and when he sighs along the inward arc of my neck
the whole world turns to jasmine and dusk.

## ii. Splendour and light

Wrapped in the white linen sheets of the hotel,
looking up at the plaster grapevines
along the edge of the ceiling
as ice-cold drops of water trail
down the wine glass on the windowsill,
we are shrouded in the smoke
of a burning ember, held
between his thumb and index finger.

*If it is inspiration you seek,* he says, *you have only to breathe.*

So the nicotine haze
and late night heat
fill the blood vessels
pulsing
beneath my cool pale skin.

*Imagine,* says he, *the  colour red.*
*Tell me what you see.*

Merlot in cut crystal
*the shade of bruised rose*
when it touches the tongue
*it enters the heart*
with the fire of the dawn.

*Yes.  Now.  Follow me.  Trust—yes—trust me.*

And as a star falls, just before the dark can give way to dawn
he leads me to the foot of a Saracen tower on a hill
and we look over the fields of sandy ground and sunflowers,
over the dark green trees and the dun grey river of road
that leads to the ivory tombs of the distant cemetery.

I shiver and he offers me a black cloak
drawn from the air. He shelters me with one arm
while pointing out the fading constellations,
naming the streets of his childhood.


At the song of the lark, at the turn of the earth toward the sun,
he flinches but smiles. I take his hand, and my soul,
a spider's web of stars and glittering tears
begins to smoulder
alongside his mourning
for lost splendour and light.

iii. Your cerise lips

On the dawn of the third day we reach Marseilles
and he takes me to the wavering edge of *Golfe du Lion*
he takes me by the hand,
he leads me up to the knees
into the sea.

He catches up jewelled starfish
and casts them into my hair.

He crowns my head
with branching coral.

He places a single pearl
in the cleft of my collar bone.

Miraculously, it remains,
its sea-foam sheen catching up the light
with my every breath.
Opalescence, shimmering with the sounds
drawn from the ringed column
that cages my voice.

*You are too romantic, mon cherie*
sighs he.
*It is only the sea.*

iv. And seashell hips

At midday of the third day, we return to the village
built into the side of a hill, the village of stone houses
with tangerine shutters and streets of soft shadows
that will shield us from the unrelenting sun.

We stop at the fountain
in the centre of the stone star
in the centre of the village.

To our left stands the church
with its lilies and candlelit solace,
guarded by Michael and his host of armoured angels.

To our right stands the bakery
with its warm bread and fresh coffee.

He leans over the fountain,
bowing to Poseidon caught in the rock. He catches
water in his cupped hands and tilts it into my mouth.
The angels of the church watch and sigh
and curse their stone hearts and hands and eyes.

*Shall I write sonnets for your cerise lips*
*and seashell hips?*
asks he
*Or shall I merely take thee*
*ever further with me?*

## v. Further, and further still

And then. He leads me into Hell.

Inevitable, you are thinking. How could she be so naïve?

Wait. Listen to me. All is not as you believe:

Hell is not in the bowels of the Earth,
but high up in the hills of Provence,
beneath the hawks who survey the cultivated rows
of orchards/boneyards/vineyards.

Hell lies sanctified in a place
where only the things named by men may live,
and the land is all sand and heat and tenacious green.

It is water, not fire, that is cruel, for I hear
the sound of a river with every turn of my head
but there is no water, only rock
and red grapes that I am too tired to steal.

He leads me along winding blacktop roads,
their serpentine switch-backing leaving me
spinning, their tarry haze lingering in my lungs.

And I am caught in the dreamscape-prison
of valleys and mountains, vines and heavens.
Forevermore, I will dream dreams that scatter at the dawn
shatter at the singing of the lark.
I will dream only to wake far from this place
and despair
as I fail to remember how thirst burns,
how my once *peau de soie* skin burns,
how glittering tears in starlight
burn.

*Further, and further still.*

On a silent night, I dream
of shining wet streets, all oily and black,
spilling their waste into gutter-rivers
on which chapbooks, books of verse,
books of hours and hours and hours
all sail to the sea.

I dream of ripped bindings,
of thread exposed
like the broken sinews
in the knee of a shot deer.
I dream
of torn words
sinking into puddles
of ink and mud. I dream
of tarry blood, lurid taillights.

Awake at 4 A.M., I pour whisky
into a tumbler, toss it back
and drift into dreams
of a saviour,
of a stranger who wraps
a wool blanket
around my shoulders
after a shipwreck,
who holds my palms up, open
to let the rain fall into them.

dear Persephone—

it wasn't the pomegranate, was it?
c'mon, confess, 'cause the jig is up.

it was words, words, words
as delicious
as those tart-sweet seeds, wasn't it?

and who could blame Hades?
what with your hair of golden August wheat,
your slender ankles. (or so says Zeus,
ever the exonerator of injustices
he files away under Indiscretions: Minor)

O! Thoughtless Child who unleashed
the wrath of winter upon us all, who ensures
April is ever the cruellest month—
you never did tell the truth to you mother,
never did consider that you owed her that, at least.

so it's fallen to me, the one with the sticky fingers,
mind strumming like the strings of a lute,
and no more moral sense than a cat
to set things right. because I know what he wrote.
I have those words right here in my pocket,
his postcard poetry, fatal and suave:

i.
*Your eyes are a window that looks upon*
*a tornado: shattering glass, dark howling*

ii.
*Your skin is honey running hot, your laugh*
*a river of larks rising; I love you*
*more than sand loves the waves of the ocean*

iii.

*I would give you a cloak of night stars*
*if we were both gods among cloudbursts and light,*
*if we could be other than what we are*

38      iv.

*Your absence is the dark of a sky*
*swallowed whole, that ocean cry*


serious fellow, isn't he?
must go with the territory.
but if you ever wonder,
dear Persephone,
how your mother spends her winters
while you preside over Eurydice, etc.,
it looks something like this:


a lone woman
on a frostbitten bridge
of black latticed iron,
shredding each ink-line penned
by her daughter's lover,
letting them sweep and drift
like feathers
down
to the fractured ice,
where words
are reduced
to the playthings
of currents.

Dear Cara,

As children, we slept in beds set
within kicking distance. So close
we once stuck a line of red tape
down the middle of the cold
concrete floor of our room:
your space was a tucked-in bed,
your shoes neatly arranged beneath.
Mine, a hopelessly sentimental disarray
of favourite books and blankets
and gossamer butterflies made by Auntie Kate.

Three days into our border dispute
you threw a paperclip onto my side,
snide that I'd never notice it in the mess.
In response, I lunged at you in a mad rage,
the fight not breaking up until our mother
pried us apart and sentenced us to kneel
in the neat rows of her garden, weeding.

These days, the space that separates us
feels as vast as the red cliffs of the Grand Canyon.
Everything that matters—memory, trust, anger—
spirals down into its chasms.
Every day, you write to me in the afternoon.
The letters always begin with "I am fine. How are you?"
I am given stacks of these missives
each time I enter from the far side of the glass,
joining your world with its smoothed-down
predictability of bleached sheets and pills in paper cups.

39

I visit faithfully, always carrying
the letters I have written for you,
bound up in red string and weighing heavily
in the tattered satchel of my ragged bohemian life.
Today, I sit on the edge of your bed
and pull the string loose, full of blind hope
that I can cause all that we have lost,
or wasted, to be tossed back lightly to us,
like the echo of laughter among precipices.

It was a small book, an awkward 5x5 dimension,
bound in pearl-white vinyl and kept on the end-table
on which the lamp made from a twisted tree branch always sat.

The photos were faded, not with the passage of time,
but with the pallor of another era, the Kodachrome
flash-flaring the indigo satin of the bridesmaid's dress
into the dreary blue of a Sunday afternoon.

41

I kept from her, always, my childhood disappointment
that her gown ended just above her ankles, rather than
sweeping out behind her in a train as voluminous and glittering
as a mermaid's tail, all saltwater and sun; I kept from her
my longing for intricately stitched patterns of pearls
in place of—nothing. Only plain white synthetic,
made a dingy ivory by the film that snapped up that day
and shaped it into a catalogue of predictable events:
the departure from her father's house, the walk down the aisle,
the exchange of rings, the signing of the register.

The story ends with the two of them standing side-by-side,
my father in a dark-coloured suit and sober tie,
their arms linked, their smiles fixed. Behind them
is the gnarled taupe trunk of a tree, and behind that
a blank yellowish blur of field that would soon be a parking lot.

April twenty-fifth in Alberta. In a month, that tree would have been
dropping with cherry blossoms, humming with dozens of bees.

As it was, it stood pale and skeletal, like any starved creature
after a long white winter it doesn't quite believe has broken.

With the rain gusting in fish-silver sheets
beyond the other side of the candlelit café,
my aunt tells me how she travelled by ship
from Montreal through the Panama Canal
around the Cape of Good Hope to London
and, still restless, hitchhiked from Calais
to Damascus; she says: *you & I share
an inheritance of wanderlust* and we laugh
and set the room to ringing with our wine glasses.

Later, we speak of our grandmothers,
that procession of three
who must have lived with a madness
under their skin
caused by seeing the same scene undulating
each morning and every night,
caused by being born on the edge of a prairie coulee
knowing, in their bones, they'd be buried
on the edge of its shadow.

Later still, we speak of how her-father-my-grandfather
did see the world, telling us both as children how
he'd once had a room with a view of the Vatican
as he, a hastily trained army medic, plunged
his hands into gore, feeling muscle and breath
grasp frantically for life under his hands.
*A failure of hydraulics,* he once said.
*That moment without end when the blood ceases
to circulate, and you are left to seal
the lids of the empty jars of eyes.*

She and I stop speaking, and I watch her slip
into memory, to the time before my birth,
and I suddenly wonder if the cornea of the eye
becomes a map of its final view, and whether
it is true that at death we turn inward and see
the vast un-scrolling of our own lives, and smile.

i.

Fog bodies of breath all around them—
standing among winter wraiths,
4 kids wait for the rumble and black exhaust
of the school bus. When it arrives,
they'll clamber up the steps
to the grooved plastic floor, slick with ice
and vicious laughter if you slip. Only 2 heaters,
both at the back of the bus, where the big kids sit,
the girls with shellacked hair and foxtails dangling
from their purses, the boys in black leather jackets,
cigarettes in their pockets, one earring
in the ear that means you're not gay. It's 2 weeks
till Xmas and 2 of the kids waiting are grade 4 girls
whose hair brittles with glittering frost
as their own breath spreads
from their lips and grows icy as death.
*This is what we'll look like*
*when we're old hags at death's door,* 1 girl whispers
to the other and they both giggle till tears freeze
the thick of their black lashes together. They blink,
crinkling ice in their eyes as they look long
down the country road.
                                    Where it ends is a field,
and in the field, shadow-coyotes lope along
in the slow red dawn. One leaps, lunges.
                                    The girls know
something has been killed, a mouse or snow hare,
and their lashes freeze again as the 2 boys
jostle and shout *guts* and *balls* and laugh too loud.

The girl who whispered looks away. Before her
are paper birches, white in their winter weight of snow. The
wet black of the gnarls in their bark
makes her think of the newspapers that morning,
and her mind grows full of the headlines, their cheap ink staining
her from the inside.

ii.

That morning, the girl who whispered saw the photos
of Ethiopian children and cracked orange earth.

44      Her mother turned the page quickly, hoping
none of her children would see, plunked down
bowls of porridge before each of them and issued her usual
winter weather warning:
*Flesh Will Freeze in Under a Minute!*

Then she bundled all of them all up
in scarves and mitts and parkas and boots and hoods
and sent them trudging off.

iii.

Waiting in the white,
the girl who whispered about death
looks long in the distance
and pictures the dirt and distended bellies,
remembers the stories
that different branches of her own family tell
of the dirty thirties, the potato famine, the hunger winter.

She remembers the history class on immigrants
they had last week at school,
and how they were sent home to draw up a family tree,
everyone talking on the bus
about the tragedies that brought their parents
or grandparents or great-grandparents here.

And it all begins to fit together,
makes her head feel as heavy
as the limbs of the birch trees laden with snow,
this feeling of why her elderly aunt
keeps three freezers filled with sides of beef,
of why her mother glues 4-leaf clovers
to the front door each summer, of why broken chairs
and china and waste-not-want-not rags proliferate in the
creaking gloom of her grandmother's basement,
the reek of fear rising like oily smoke and reaching out
like the clutching, empty hands of babies
born with brittle bones.

Lie flat. Let the dead grass impress into your skin
the pattern of itself waving in the wind.

We could crack open like birch trees on fire,
anchored as we are in the veins of bone-dry creek beds,
our hearts curling up like the thirsting leaves
of elm and poplar, their edges like hands
praying to this stretch of hot blue infinity.

Do you feel the spin of the earth on its axis at night?
A girl dancing the tarantella.

Do you feel the dustbowl rim of summer stretching out?
This swath of waiting as flat as the horizon.

Until the sky turns absinthe green,
and an eerie calm whorls itself
into a throat of howling black.

And then we run, coil under low ceilings. Listen
for the absolute black panic of shattering glass,
hear only each liquid thud of breath and blood.

46

This place is sour gas burn-off,
alkali, and sky-blue bisected by
black cables and their electric deadly hum,
their Titan's claws gripping
down into layers of soil,
their skeletons shrugging off thunder,
the forked tongues of lightning.

Once, the swoop-down of a summer storm
snapped a cable loose with a single slap
and a line writhed free, hissing like a cobra.

The child who caught it
became the town's cautionary tale:
grasp a live wire, and a charcoal highway
will snake right through you, your heart turning
igneous black while your skin remains perfectly intact,
pale as that of a marble-carved god, even as the smoke
of your burnt blood curls away from you, frail fingers,
seeking, supplicating.

Crossing at the pedestrian crossing,
the car skidded, screeched, stopped.
I looked up, rolled my eyes,
glanced at my watch. 5:30 P.M.

48     So I know exactly where I was.

Though it was Mikey who found her the next morning.

A pot of water was sitting on the gas burner.
Only half of the potatoes had been peeled,
the ground beef left out on the counter.

The 5:30 dinnertime routine.

He dialled 911. It was the only number he
could think to call, blurting out
to the woman who answered:
*Thank God the gas wasn't left on.*

And it's right there that the imagination
begins to play magic tricks, steps into
the hollow wounds clawed out of us
by the instances in which
we are not where we needed to be.

Imagination conjures up bagpipe music playing
as the sun set, and one of grandma's antique tea cups,
cracked, sitting beside a completed crossword puzzle.

It whispers that it was a relief for her,
after the last round of tests,
to relinquish the struggle, the constant
vigilance against signs of failure
as sure to come as the breaking bones
when a bird crashes into glass.

Imagination makes her last gesture a lifted hand
that a loved one caught in the sudden haze of pain
as her whole body became a whetstone,
sparks flaring in her veins, freeways of nerves
turning on edge, her eyesight blurring
as if a thread had been slipped through her tear duct
and tightened, tightened.

Then, snapped.

dear mom & dad,

Neither of you would remember this day,
the day of my first memory.

50      I can only tell you, now, with that day long past,
and one of you ashes among roses.

The memory is of the sun rising: dawn
in what could only be the first week of May.

Dad getting into his black pickup,
his white construction hat on the dash.

The huh-huh-huh of the engine
turning over as he turned the key.

Mom in the kitchen, mixing pancake batter,
a jar of honey on the counter.

The buds on the trees spiralling open,
the cherry blossoms and lilacs
that meant my birthday would be soon:

gifts tied up with red ribbons,
chocolate cake with a coin for luck
beneath the slice meant for me.

No memory, yet, of how birthday
also meant pain and blood and fear;
no younger brother, yet, to teach me
the meaning of Caesarean and share.

Only the sun rising with that intensity of red
meant to make sailors take warning.

I never asked for this. At least, not exactly this.
This figure, this half-a-moon curve of abdomen
so foreign and unfamiliar it almost has nothing
to do with me, an event taking place inside
that bears no resemblance to this daily waking life.

A fist or a foot bubbling up against the surface.
The panic I felt the first few times, as if I were
seeing evidence of some wild creature there,
the back of a tiny whale as it rose up against the skin
of his private ocean, not surfacing, but there, skimming
just under the air, in the roiling waters.

And me, feeling not so much like an ocean. More like
a worn book with several pages torn out
and an abundance of indecipherable phrases.

# The Annunciation

(1465, Antonello da Messina)

This time:
no angel
no golden light
no dove
no lily.

52

Only Mary,
her head covered
by a coarse grey cloth,
her alabaster face
and soft mouth
set in contrast
to the blackness
behind her.

A book is open before her, its pages
curving as her hand curves up
in a gesture—is it greeting
or abeyance?—meant for the one
who stands
where I now stand.

And then the announcement:
*The gallery will close in fifteen minutes.*

And I, in place of an angel,
depart and do not return.

She awakes, this time, not to the song
of the lark outside her open window
but to a stranger who thrusts
a stem of lilies at her
and she stares at them,
heart racing in panic
not at what the stranger says
but at his nakedness,
seen through the slit
in the side of his tunic.

The day before
she had spent tending to the orchard,
white and pink apple blossoms
falling into her hair.
She had crushed herbs for medicine
with a mortar and pestle
in the quiet kitchen of her mother
while, in the other room,
there was talk of her betrothal.

Reading that night,
she fell asleep on her narrow cot
and dreamt she was an Athenian owl,
her voice a part of the night,
haunting even the brightest stars.

The memory of that will fade. She knows.

There is nothing for her now
but daylight and the peculiar silence
that surrounds one,
one who hears angels
then hears them no more.

## Bacchus as a Baby

*(Wealth.* 1630, Simon Vouet)

A woman with wide arcing shoulders
and a round profile
holds steady a small child with her
plump long-nailed hands.

54
She does not look at him
but at the cherry-cheeked cherub hugging her dress
and lifting up two necklaces
(one of pearl, one of gold)
in a style that would pinch
the thin skin of the woman's throat.

The child, slightly drunk,
points at the woman's crown
of grapevine leaves, her dress of satin waves
washing around them,
an orchard of blossoms
in a midsummer night's storm.

At her naked feet
sits a Grecian Urn
and an open book of wine-splashed pages,
weeping merlot
and love.

is to be a girl who is not even a part of the painting,
but someone who sees herself, unseen, in one of the houses
sewing a hem in pale yellow light; it is to be a child down
by the bank of the river, fishing in bare feet. Out of sight,
but present, as the stillness of the water plays with the light,
embraces its warmth, the two elements making mirror-images
of houses along the bank, of the spring trees in leaf.

Out of sight, we become the bridge above the canal
and the horse's good-luck shoes clattering
across the cobbles, we become the constant splashing
of the mill as the summer sky above reveals itself in whorls
of blue oil, as thick as fingerprints, against which
we can press our own fingertips to feel the perfection
of surface tension, the hum of it like a voice
ready for song, a dragonfly upon a pond.

55

i. a monk, a whore, a white horse

*Pont Neuf:*

1578 the new bridge begins with Henri III placing the first stone after a funeral, fumbling with his rosary beads, calling it the Bridge of Tears and walking off into the League of Troubles ... 1607 Pont Neuf is opened by Henri IV and Marie de Medici; after they leave the prostitutes-booksellers-beggars-hawkers arrive, knights on white chargers clatter across, thieves with knives up their sleeves slit throats for pennies, poets-playwrights-monks-magicians cast spells and sparks ... 1614 the bronze likeness of Henri IV watches them all from his high horse and *La Samarataine* pours forth water beneath the bas-relief of Christ meeting the Samaritan at Jacob's Well

1790 *La Revolution*: that series of slicings, bloodied blades, Henri IV's statue pushed-pulled-smashed-melted: copper for cannons, gore for gutters ... 1813 *La Samaritaine* destroyed ... 1818 Henri and horse re-built ... 1927 a different kind of *La Samaritaine* can sell you everything and anything ... 1985 Christo wraps the lamps / the vaults / the arches / the esplanade of the Vert-Galant and the three hundred and eighty four mascarons in woven polyamide and asks you to imagine golden sandstone silk and for ten dazzling days everyone walks on the weaving ... 2004 you and I arrive, made stupid from the relentless sun, our eyes glazing under the shadows of our ultraviolet blue shades ...

or, *Pont Neuf*:

> my hand a white skein of jointed bones
> against the lines of the iron lamp post

> my body all kingfisher angles
> leaning out across the parapet

> my hair uncoiling on my neck,
> Mnemosyne above dark waters

> and you, rocking back on your heel
> your eye one with the camera's eye

> the cradle of Paris,
> swinging.

ii. mass

*Look for the bronze plate set in the paving stone in front of the cathedral. Place your*
*feet on this plate. It is* point zéro, *the place from which the distances between all*
*other places in france are measured. this is the still silent heart of paris, the city's*
*past, present, future.*

This is the long line of tourists waiting to climb the bell tower
This is the attack of pigeons seeking crumbs
This is the archway leading into the cathedral
This is the counter-clockwise crawl past madonnas and martyrs

I see flashes flaring, phosphorous light bouncing off stone ladies
I see nuns kneeling amid the ruckus and Christ looking sad
I see Americans drawling *so this is notra damn cáthedraaal*
I see my own feet crossing over cobbles, passing under shadows

The masses gather here, a Babel for the bell-tower
The Catholics gather here, kneeling, hands clasped
The tourists gather here, in love with demi-monde
The gargoyles leer here, alongside the silent saints

*And struck by the stunning profound useless beauty of it all, of measuring distances*
*and illuminating flying buttresses, of staining glass and burning incense and*
*arranging flowers, would you, would I, trade places with the generations of builders*
*who made this place? Could you, could I, surrender our modern conveniences (literacy,*
*say, or the smoking engines of cars) to architect a faith into being, our mouths*
*reciting Latin prayers as gothic spires aspire and bones rattle in shallow catacombs?*

iii. sunflowers sparrows shadows

Between shadow's edge and end of island
the sun gathers a garden of sparrows.

Everyone takes sparrows for granted.
Their bright black eyes and brown feathers,
their hopping flights.

The sparrows do not care that they are taken for granted.

We sit on green benches under trees,
a trash can every twelve paces, and wait
to know what to do next.

Hungry, we leave the sparrows and pass through
a market of lavender, roses, sunflowers.

As a hawk dives down through the sky
we pass by a building
with stones the colour of dead fish flesh
that sucks the warmth from our skin.

Later we learn that this palace
was named death's antechamber,
aristocrats waiting there to be carted
across the cobbles to *Place de la Concorde*.

I say to you: I remember
how the executioners
had to keep moving the guillotine,
every neighbourhood complaining
eventually
about the stench,
the sensation of iron and salt,
a madness in the throat.

dear Nike—

Oh, to write you an ode, a sonnet, a rock song.

60       To do justice to the magnificent irony of the iron
that binds your stony wings in flight, to how skilfully
they've pieced each fragment of your broken body together
in a doomed attempt to resurrect you.

Ah, dearest Winged Victory of Samothrace,
you are nothing but an idle icon now, and a headless one at that,
and I know that writing to you is about as streetwise as writing poems
to skylarks and nightingales, so I figure it's time I hit the road
and if you miss me when I'm gone, let's just say it's like that song
sung by the guy with the limo and the leather jacket—
*Look, I've gotta go. Yeah, I'm running out of change.*
*There's a lot of things ... if I could, I'd rearrange*

Ricochet shot: cracked dawn of white waking,
shaken from sugarplums to gasoline
and guns one crystalline morning of blood-
ice splinters, a halo of red spreading

as we sank to our knees in the clearing,
imagining the poachers hack-sawing
a split-seam through fur and throat, then gripping
his antlers and leering. our father swore

and spat, dragged the carcass to our garage,
spent the day scraping, hunter's blades slitting
through skin, muscle, sinew and bone. Carving

cold sustenance from rage. the frosted heart
in a field of snow we placed. all night, the wolves'
echo-howling hunger sang of fallen grace.

My mother raised swans that my father killed
and made us eat. white down, hot water, blood.

How I hated it, hated it, hated it.
I wanted deer to eat cherries from my hand,
the hunger in my belly to be stalled
by milk and honey, no need for this

elemental need: salt and iron on the tongue,
the rust-red stain of it yoked to the rhythm
of every dance, every poem, every song:
ta-da, ta-da, ta-da, ta-da, ta-da.

A magician's trick, a sleight of hand:
the slicing thump of axe through flesh,
severing life from death, word from sound
and fury splayed and splattered in raw air.

No, I'm from that other place, the one
that did not give the world
jazz or revolution or pulp fiction,
that did not make famous
Hiroshima and Nagasaki.

Yes, that other place, the one so cold,
so vast, it could be a Tolstoy novel.
Only it isn't.

So, what am I doing here?
Up to my ankles in red Devon mud,
the rain making the sky a haze,
the rain so ceaseless you'd think
this whole island
was trying to be the new Atlantis.

That other place, when it was hazy,
it was hazy with blizzards. Or it was a sky
cut to ribbons
by birch and elm
whose winter arms
were thin as blades.
It was colours
sharp as struck flint—
flame of tamarack,
black needle of open water
down the midline of a white river.

At night, I dream of tundra
in perpetual twilight, surreal fields
of sunset-glazed ice, of polar bears
whose roars
and tears
are my home.

Trees stand like de-mobbed soldiers, battered and gnarled.
They dream of the life that went astray on the harsh winds
back in the days when their new leaves shot up in hope of heat.

The darling buds of May? A midsummer night's dream,
or the bleak mid-winter? Who can say, in this landscape
of meshed elements, seasons smudged together?

A soup of stupor and timelessness, it drowns
the childhood idea that eternity is a castle of white stone
standing in a pool of golden light, it makes me see

that time is as malleable as air, and air is as palpable as water,
that water brings the sky down to stone and skin, and everything
is made as slippery as the roots of the trees that grip the ground
of the village ruins as the sun sinks under a blurred horizon of hills
that look like overturned bowls. A lone oak tree in the distance
rising up, pointing the way, a shadow hung in of scarves of mist.

Sight a blackbird in a winter tree,
sunlight on the fallow fields beyond it. You long

to live forever. Death. It is not close to you,
you who are neither ill nor old. But there death is. You
see it hanging in the naked branches. The blackbird edges
along it; you see death waiting, already, in the fields
for the seedlings that will be planted in spring. Even the sunlight

has been robbed of being infinite, divine. Reduced, now,
to a lengthy explosion, a set of chemical reactions
bound to reach equilibrium one day.

                    By then, you
will be long gone. Done and dusted. Angel? Or simply absent?
You flip coins, call heads or tails on the matter:
                              does it matter?
Either way, you long to live forever. Either way, you lose.

dear Eros—

how funny it is that your name
sounds so much like *errors*.

66     a wilful, naughty boy with wild wavy hair
and a twist of mischief in your smile—
*that* is how they've sculpted you.

Oh, and the trouble they've blamed you for—
launching a thousand ships,
kissing cold lover's poisoned lips.

if only they could see you as I do;
a god of rain, not of raining arrows. it is you
who brings the heavens sloping down into the ocean,
who lets the sky fall, gently, on fields and forests.

they refuse to see it, preferring instead
to make themselves into sieves, a hollow mesh
of flesh and tears that they mistake
for the strikes of a million arrows.

and now, they've turned you to stone.
as if they are gorgons with streaming snake-hair
hissing out the last of their desires and despair.

they have placed you on a plinth in a gallery.

as if Love is an artefact,
a work to be studied. or, worse,
surrounded by flocks of tourists
squawking like seagulls.

because the coffee needs brewing and the cat needs brushing and the birds
need feeding and the bread needs kneading and the email needs reading  and
because there is a bus to catch and books to unlatch and letters to send and
old fences to mend and because the forms must be signed on the dotted
line and things must be said while you still have the time and because you
have dreams of a lizard, painted pink, who eats up the earth with a grin and
a wink, and what is the point of a poem in a world on the brink—what do
you think?—in the midst of catastrophe who's going to miss this simple
apostrophe?

Dangerous thing, this echoing of voices
being swallowed whole
by a long throat of damp stone.

The first fairy tales of childhood
always warned of wells,
of foolish boys and selfish maids
who fell into the brackish black.

Essential, however, was this risk—
so necessary, the wheeling up of water
with its ungraspable clarity. A contradiction—
the opaque eloquence of the well,
the transparent need that is thirst.

The silence that follows the clattering fall.

68

dear Mnemosyne—

how they've scattered you.
I wouldn't have thought it possible,
if I hadn't seen it all with my own eyes.
you. daughter of sky and earth.

cheeky monkeys, they stole you
from the elements and impressed your face
on every statue, coin, canvas. gave you shape
as saints, artists, despots. unknown soldiers,
but never their mothers. and some of them,
the worst of them, began to believe
They Were Gods.

and you? you have been consigned
to silence, the silence of a locked
*musée des beaux arts* after hours. it almost
makes me laugh, how these galleries contain
all the hopes and all the fears of all the years,
try to lash them into order  but we both know
they are nothing but an endless variation
on Pandora's box. it almost makes me laugh.
but then I hear you, crying out,
calling to your nine daughters.

they never answer. I do not know why.

this much, at least, I can tell you:

I hear rumours of them daily on my travels.
tourists whisper of them in St. Paul's or the Uffizi,
gasp over them before the works of Boticelli and Canova,
sigh for them in the Ode to Joy, Citizen Kane,
Where the Streets Have No Name.

I do not know if they can hear you call, for no one,
not even me (ever the itinerant and impertinent),
can find them. it is as if their feet have been
rooted in place, like Daphne's in her final plea,
as if they have vanished into clouds of laurel leaves.

so this I will promise you: I will seek them out for you,
seek them among the labyrinths of books and artefacts,
seek them and bring them home to you,
even if it takes a donkey's age, and offers no rest for me
(though I am far from wicked). I will seek them for you
even if it means skating the surface
of the deepest of all rivers, risking its slipperiness
and depths, risking the river that, if sipped,
will turn me to sunlight and ice.

A still life, with books:
a counter-spell for portents
found in the blood of dead rabbits,
the dark blush of bruised tulips

or in the pages on a splintered brown table,
or the shallow clink of a quill in an inkwell.

I'd be hard-pressed to explain why the myths of ancient Greece mean so much to me, although in many respects, it's hardly surprising. I spent my childhood longing to be anywhere other than where I was, but Europe in general, and Greece in particular, felt like the *somewhere* I most wanted to be. The intensity of the sunlight, the enduring lives of cities, ruins, and stories—these were exciting alternatives to Alberta winters and the dreariness of my school-day routine. Like the traveller, I've gotten pretty good at vanishing acts since then; I've also learned that some things— memory, love, and, above all, the unexpected complications that are the stuff of mythologies—are not things one would wish to escape, even if it were possible to do so (which it isn't). I've added some notes here in the hope that they will add to your enjoyment of the poems.

Hermes, the son of Zeus and Maia, is the trickster figure of Greek mythology. On the day of his birth, Hermes accomplished an astonishing number of things: he flattered a tortoise into crawling into his hands, then killed her and used her shell to make the first lyre; he stole fifty of Apollo's cattle and then butchered two of them to sacrifice to the gods; and, when confronted by Apollo over his crimes, he talked his way out of getting in trouble before the court of the gods at Olympus. As if this weren't enough, he also played the lyre so beautifully that Apollo was overcome with the desire to possess the instrument, so he gave Hermes a travelling staff, dominion over cattle and flocks, and influence over the Bee Women of Parnassus (who prophesy if they are fed wild honey, and who lie if they go unfed) in exchange for it. Zeus appointed him as the herald of the gods, and he was also given the task of leading the souls of the deceased to the Underworld. There is no basis in Greek mythology for the traveller; she is pure invention.

Dionysus is the Greek god of wine, revelry, and the good life. Maenads ("the maddened ones") were his female followers, who reputedly worked themselves into a frenzy through ecstatic dances and could become dangerously violent. Scholars argue that there is little evidence to support this reputation, although one cycle of myths relates how the women of Thrace, following Dionystic rites, tore the poet Orpheus limb from limb.

Chronos is a personification of time (not to be confused with Kronos, the king of the Titans and father of Zeus).

Hera is Zeus's wife, and the goddess of women and marriage. Because of her ever-philandering husband, she devoted much energy to taking revenge on Zeus's many lovers/conquests/victims. In one myth, for instance, she slipped snakes into the bed of the sleeping Herakles, who was the lovechild of Zeus and the mortal woman Alkmene. In another tale, the mortal woman Io, a priestess of Hera, attracted the attention of Zeus, who turned her into a white cow to prevent Hera from becoming suspicious. When Hera discovered Zeus's deception, she caused a gadfly to sting Io relentlessly, driving her from continent to continent to escape it. The same tale also relates how the peacock, associated with Hera, came to have "eyes" in its tail: Hera arranged to have the many-eyed Argos guard the white cow Io from Zeus so that Hera could ascertain whether Zeus is Io's lover. Zeus then commanded Hermes to murder Argos, and Hera partially avenged Argos's death by placing his eyes in the tail of her favourite bird.

Jan Lievens was a Dutch painter whose teacher, Pieter Lastman, also taught Rembrandt. *Portrait of the Artist's Mother* is a part of the collection at Wilton House in Salisbury, UK.

Lorenzo Monaco ("Lorenzo the Monk") is a late Gothic / early Renaissance painter who was based in Florence. *The Annunciation* is part of the collection at the Galleria dell'Accademia in Florence.

Fra Angelico was a monk and early Renaissance painter who was based at the San Marco monastery in Florence from 1436 to 1495. Many of the frescoes he painted in the cells there remain today, as does the splendid fresco of *The Annunciation* at the top of the stairs that one climbs upon visiting the monastery.

Ponte Vecchio is a medieval bridge across the narrowest point of the Arno in Florence. The "other river" remembered by the traveller is the River Styx, across which Charon ferried the dead into the realm of Hades. In some stories, the failure to have a have a coin with which to pay Charon doomed the deceased person to wander along the bank of the river.

Demeter is the goddess of grains and the harvest. Her daughter Persephone was kidnapped by Hades, god of the Underworld. Demeter's grieving for her lost daughter caused the crops to fail and famine to ensue, until an agreement was reached—Persephone would stay with Hades in the Underworld for half of the year, and join her mother for the other half.

Antonello da Messina was a Renaissance painter who studied in the Netherlands and is credited with bringing oil painting to Italian art. *Virgin Annunciate* is part of the collection at the Galleria Nazionale in Palermo.

Dante Gabriel Rossetti was one of the founders (with William Holman Hunt and John Everett Millais) of the Pre-Raphaelite Brotherhood in London in 1848. *The Annunciation* is part of the collection at the Tate Britain in London.

Simon Vouet was a Baroque painter based in Paris. His painting *La Richesse* is a well known allegory of wealth and the pleasures it can offer. It is part of the collection at the Louvre in Paris.

Alfred Sisley was a French Impressionist painter, based in Paris, who concentrated primarily on painting landscapes. *View of the Canal St-Martin* (1870) is part of the collection at Musée d'Orsay in Paris.

Nike is the Greek goddess of victory. The sculpture known as *Winged Victory of Samothrace* is considered one of the three "Ladies of the Louvre" (*Venus de Milo* and the *Mona Lisa* are the other two). It was found in pieces at Rhodes in the mid-1800s, and painstakingly puzzled together, though its head and arms are still missing. The sculpture has stood atop the Daru Staircase of the Louvre since 1883.

Eros, the child of Venus and Mars (love and war), is renowned for causing mischief with his arrows (the gold-tipped ones reputed to provoke love, while the lead-tipped ones repelled it).

Mnemosyne is the daughter of Ouranos (sky) and Gaia (earth). Her name means "Memory," and she is the mother of the nine Muses.

The River Lethe is one of the five rivers of the Underworld; the souls of the dead were required to drink from it and so erase all memory of their mortal lives.

Jan Davidsz de Heem was a still-life painter of the Flemish school. He was based primarily in Utrecht and Antwerp. *Still Life with Books* is part of the collection at the Mauritshuis Museum in The Hague.

Imagine a very grateful poet, with a very generous bottle of champagne, raising a glass:

To Alice Major, for your editorial wisdom as I finalised the manuscript. Your incisive insights, paired with your unfailing kindness and generosity cannot be praised highly enough: thank you.

To Peter Midgley, for believing in this book from the beginning. Your enthusiasm, patience, and sense of humour have helped transform these poems into that wonderful gift: a book.

To everyone at the University of Alberta Press who contributed, and, indeed, continues to contribute to making this *dear Hermes…* a success—to Alan Brownoff for a splendid design, Mary Lou Roy for attending to details, Cathie Crooks and Monika Igali for your marketing expertise, and Linda Cameron for overseeing it all.

To Greta Stoddart, a poetry tutor extraordinaire, and to my fellow Exeter poets—Diana Gittins, Helen Evans, Sali Mustafic, Katie Moudry, Gordon Read, Diana Hekt, Dennis Casling, Sue Proffit, Frank Hooper, Barbara Farley, Mike, Ruth Bell, Sally Douglas—for your camaraderie and willingness to your share work and your own love of poetry with me.

To Bert Almon, who was the first to read some of these poems, and encouraged me to keep writing.

To Marian, Randall, Liam, and Kyra, for your laughter, love, and Skype sessions—and, of course, your willingness to visit Britanny with me.

To Sandra, for reading so many of these poems with such enthusiasm, and to Court for sharing your photographs of Alberta landscape with me, and to both of you, for dreaming up the trip to Greece and then making it a reality.

To Liz, for the much-needed phone calls to a certain exhausted new mother, not to mention giving up Alberta's August sunshine to visit Scotland in the rainiest summer on record!

To Dad, for your insights into our heritage, and to Aunt Gloria, for your inspiring stories of your own travels and your investigations into the Norwegian side of the family.

To Rowan Fraser, for sharing your knowledge of Greek mythology, and for cheering me along whenever I wanted to quit; to Faye Hammill, for being an inspiring mentor and dear friend; to Jillian Garrett for your 200-words-a-day and for making me laugh through the good and the bad; to Colleen Addision, for being ma chère et excellente amie; to Lindsay Light, for the cookies, yoga, and general good cheer, and to Claude Kananack, for ever more good cheer; to Ann Wyatt-Smith, for many conversations shared over a crêpe (or two!); to Claire Jeavons and Mark Doidge, for your friendship and hospitality, especially your invitations to Torquay to enjoy its interesting weather; to Isabelle Charmantier and Brian Clark, for your friendship and reassurances that having a child just keeps things interesting; and to Suzanne Tailleur, for your steadfastness in the face of mythological lions and croissant-wielding conductors.

Above all, to Matthew, for his love and unceasing faith in me, and to Dashiell, for teaching me that every word we learn is a little bit of magic.

Financial support was provided by SSHRC in the form of a Postdoctoral Fellowship, for which I am profoundly grateful, and without which this manuscript could not have been completed.

A number of poems in *dear Hermes...* have appeared in other publications. I'd like to extend my appreciation to the literary magazines and journals that first published the following:

"The traveller writes from the edge of the Aegean: dear Dionysus..." *Contemporary Verse 2* 31.2 (2008): 40.

"The traveller writes from the beach in Barcelona one night: dear Chronos..." *Contemporary Verse 2* 31.2 (2008): 41.

"A Tragedy of Azure Grace." *Grain* 35.2 (Fall 2007): 16–21. [revised as "You are too romantic, mon cherie"]

"île de la cité / city of light." *Arc Poetry Magazine* 55 (Winter 2005): 45–49.

"Sea." *Other Voices: A Journal of the Literary and Visual Arts* 16.1 (2004): 47. [revised as "For the seashell girl"]

"Trio." *Grain* 30.1 (2002): 107–11. [revised as "The bear's dance"]

"Okanagan Cherry." *The New Quarterly* 21.4 (2002) 114. [revised as "Laden"]

"A Story About a Cat Named Clarence." *Room of One's Own* 24.3 (2002) 53–54.

Other Titles from The University of Alberta Press

**Demeter Goes Skydiving**

SUSAN MCCASLIN

*136 pages*

*A volume in cuRRents, a Canadian literature series*

*978-0-88864-551-7 ‖ $19.95 (T) paper*

*Poetry*

**The Office Tower Tales**

ALICE MAJOR

*264 pages*

*A volume in cuRRents, a Canadian literature series*

*978-0-88864-637-8 ‖ $19.99 (T) ePUB*

*Poetry*

**A Minor Planet for You**

*and Other Stories*

LESLIE GREENTREE

*208 pages*

*A volume in cuRRents, a Canadian literature series*

*978-0-88864-465-7 ‖ $24.95 (T) paper*

*Canadian Literature*

*dear Hermes...*

47150